ABANDONED!
Towns Without People

ROANOKE ISLAND

The Town That Vanished

by Kevin Blake

Consultant: Eric Klingelhofer
Archaeologist, First Colony Foundation
Manteo, North Carolina

BEARPORT
PUBLISHING

New York, New York

Publisher: Kenn Goin
Editor: Jessica Rudolph
Creative Director: Spencer Brinker
Design: The Design Lab
Photo Researcher: Jennifer Zeiger

Library of Congress Cataloging-in-Publication Data

Blake, Kevin, 1978–
   Roanoke Island : the town that vanished / by Kevin Blake.
      pages cm. — (Abandoned! towns without people)
   Includes bibliographical references and index.
   ISBN 978-1-62724-521-0 (library binding)—ISBN 1-62724-521-9 (library binding)
   1. Roanoke Colony—Juvenile literature. 2. Roanoke Island (N.C.)—History—16th century—Juvenile literature. I. Title.
   F229.B6193 2014
   975.6'175—dc23

2014041319

For more information, write to Bearport Publishing Company, Inc., 45 West 21st Street, Suite 3B, New York, New York 10010. Printed in the United States of America.

10 9 8 7 6 5 4 3 2 1

Contents

Abandoned

It was the early morning of August 18, 1590, and John White's ship had just reached Roanoke (ROH-uh-nohk) Island. Three years had passed since he had left a struggling **colony** on the island. Now, White was finally back. He raced up the beach, **desperate** to see everyone again.

Roanoke Island

When White reached the colony, his heart sank. Everyone was missing, including his daughter and granddaughter. White searched for clues in the **abandoned** town. The colonists' boats were missing. Their homes were gone. Worries filled White's mind. Were the Roanoke **settlers** alive or dead? What happened to them?

Roanoke Island is on the eastern coast of North America, in what is now North Carolina. Roanoke's colonists were originally from England. John White was an artist. He also served as the colony's **governor**.

England Versus Spain

Why would a group of people from England want to live on a tiny island across the Atlantic Ocean, thousands of miles from home? For Europeans in the 1500s, exploring the world meant a chance to find treasures. They hoped to build colonies and discover **natural resources**—such as gold—that could make them rich.

In the 1500s, explorers traveled the world by ship.

A ship could run into many dangers during the months it took to cross the Atlantic Ocean. A violent storm could sink the ship, or **privateers** might attack it. Privateers, who were similar to pirates, were hired by their government to attack ships from other nations.

Both Spain and England wanted to start colonies in new lands. The two countries were **rivals**. By the late 1500s, Spain had many colonies in South America and in the southern part of North America. Leaders in England wanted to compete with Spain. They planned to set up a colony on the eastern coast of North America—on Roanoke Island.

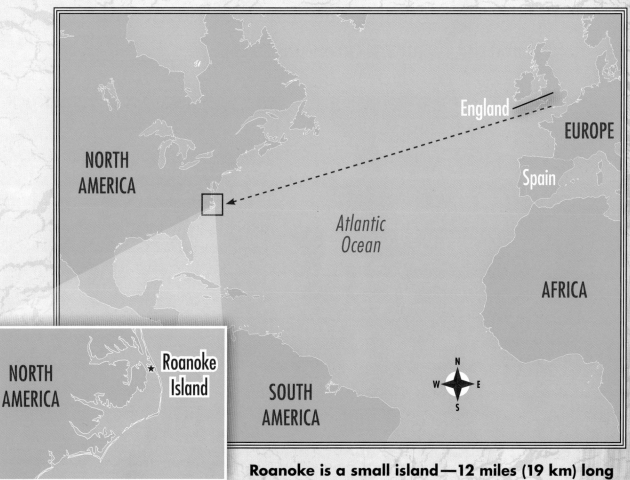

Roanoke is a small island—12 miles (19 km) long and 3 miles (4.8 km) wide.

Native Americans

In 1585, ships carrying 108 Englishmen sailed to Roanoke Island. Most of the colonists were soldiers. They built homes and a **fort** on the island. One of the colonists, however, was an artist—John White. His job was to draw pictures of the different **Native American** groups that lived in the area. These groups included the Roanoacs (ROH-uh-nohks) and the Croatoans (kroh-uh-TOH-inz).

This picture, by John White, shows a Native American village. The village includes several homes and fields of crops.

At first, the colonists and the Native Americans got along. The English soldiers weren't prepared to grow their own crops, so the Roanoacs gave them food to eat. However, the Roanoacs soon ran out of food to give. As a result, **tension** grew between the Native Americans and the colonists. Soon, the two groups became enemies.

Native Americans caught fish and grew crops, such as corn. They also hunted deer, rabbits, and bears.

Black bear

Deer

Corn

After the Roanoacs stopped giving food to the colonists, fighting broke out between the two groups. During the fighting, the colonists killed the Roanoac chief, Pemisapan.

John White Leads a New Group

The Roanoke colonists were running extremely low on supplies. So, in 1586, most of them sailed back to England. Eighteen English soldiers stayed on the island to guard the fort.

Leaders in England still wanted to build a **permanent** colony in North America, however. John White, who had been part of the first colony, helped form a new group of settlers. He became this group's governor.

White's plan was to settle on the coast of present-day Virginia, about 100 miles (161 km) north of Roanoke Island. On their way, the settlers would pick up the 18 soldiers left behind on the island. On May 8, 1587, the second group of settlers left England in three ships.

The group of settlers led by John White was made up of 118 people—92 men, 17 women, and 9 boys. Two of the women on the ship, including White's daughter Eleanor Dare, were going to have babies.

One of the settlers' ships, called the *Lion*, looked similar to this one.

Stranded on Roanoke

The dangerous trip across the Atlantic Ocean took almost three months. Finally, in July 1587, John White's group arrived at Roanoke Island. They expected to meet with the 18 English soldiers at the fort. However, when the colonists came on **shore**, they saw that the fort had been destroyed. The soldiers' homes were untouched, but all the men were gone. The only sign of the soldiers was a single skeleton lying on the dirt.

The situation only got worse from there. The captain of the *Lion* refused to take the colonists to Virginia. The settlers were **stranded** on Roanoke Island.

Most of the newly arrived colonists were completely unfamiliar with their new home, Roanoke Island.

After finding a skeleton near the destroyed fort, the colonists feared the worst—that all the soldiers were dead. The colonists then talked to the Croatoans, who said the Roanoacs had killed the soldiers.

Disaster Strikes

The colonists did their best to survive on Roanoke Island. They planned to start building some homes, but it didn't take long before disaster struck. One day, an English settler named George Howe was alone on the beach, looking for crabs to cook and eat. A group of Roanoac **warriors** spotted him. The warriors wanted revenge for the killing of their chief by the earlier colonists. The Native Americans shot several arrows into Howe's body. He was killed instantly.

The Roanoacs and the English were enemies. However, the colonists were friends with the Croatoans.

A Native American holding a bow, which is used to shoot arrows

When John White found out about Howe's death, he tried to make peace with the Roanoacs. Unfortunately, the Native Americans refused to talk with him. White and the other settlers were afraid. Would the Roanoacs try to attack and kill them, too?

Native American warriors often gathered around a fire after a battle.

Help!

The colonists were growing desperate. They worried about a Roanoac **ambush**. In addition, their food supply was running low. There was also a new member of the colony to feed and protect. On August 18, White's daughter gave birth to a girl. The baby, named Virginia Dare, was the first English baby born in the **New World**.

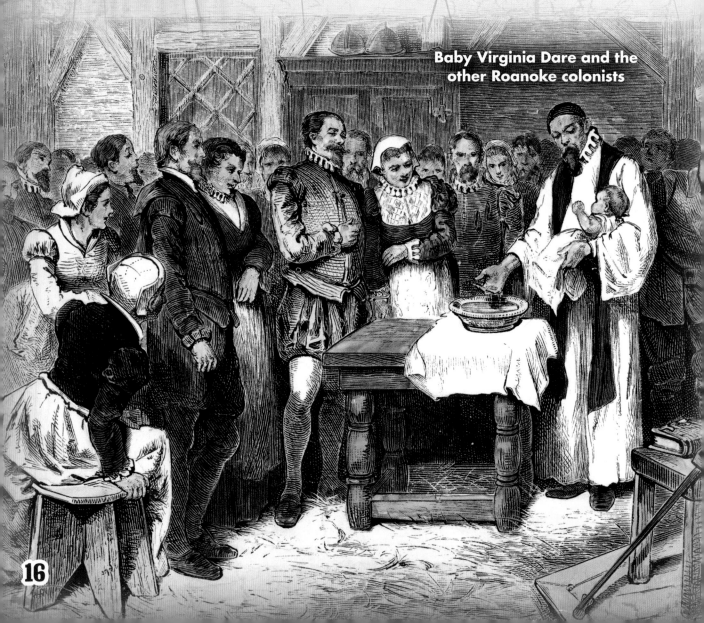

Baby Virginia Dare and the other Roanoke colonists

The Croatoans could not provide food for the colony, so the settlers would need help from England if they were going to survive. They begged White to return to England and bring back food and other supplies. On August 27, 1587, just five weeks after arriving at Roanoke, White left. He promised to return in six months.

This picture, drawn by White, shows how Native Americans cooked fish. The colonists were not skilled at growing, catching, or gathering food.

Before he left, White left instructions for the colonists. If they decided to leave the island, they should carve the name of their new location into a tree. If they had been attacked by Roanoacs, the colonists should put a cross above the name.

Stranded in England

Unfortunately, White went back to England at the worst possible time. Spain and England were at war. The two countries fought many battles at sea. English leaders ordered that all ships had to be used to help battle the Spanish. There were no ships left to bring supplies to Roanoke!

A battle at sea between English and Spanish ships

White searched for someone who could take him back to Roanoke. Finally, in 1590—almost three years after he had left the island—White met a group of English privateers who agreed to take him there. It was his only chance. He loaded the ship with supplies and left for Roanoke, hoping to see his family again.

While White was away from Roanoke Island, he had no way to communicate with the colonists. He was **frantic** to know if his daughter and granddaughter were still alive.

Mysterious Clues

In August 1590, the English privateer ship reached the seacoast near Roanoke. White and several members of the ship's crew got into a small boat and rowed toward the island. As they rowed, the crew sang songs to get the attention of the colonists on land. There was no response.

The group reached shore on the morning of August 18—Virginia's third birthday. White eagerly looked for his family. He found no one, but he saw mysterious clues. The colonists' boats and homes were gone. There were fresh footprints in the dirt. The letters "CRO" were carved into the bark of a tree. Nearby, the word "CROATOAN" was carved in a wooden gatepost. However, there was no cross carved anywhere.

Because there was no cross carved into the tree or the gatepost, White believed the settlers had not been attacked. He thought perhaps they had safely left the colony to get help from their friends, the Croatoans.

John White points to a word carved into a wooden gatepost.

This picture shows what the tree John White found might have looked like.

What Happened?

The Croatoans lived on an island 50 miles (80 km) south of Roanoke called Croatoan Island. The privateers agreed to sail to the island so White could look for the missing colonists. On the way, however, a powerful storm prevented the ship from getting close to the island.

Croatoan Island (below) is now called Hatteras Island. Dangerous storms often occur near the islands off the North Carolina coast. There have been so many shipwrecks in this area that it is nicknamed the Graveyard of the Atlantic.

The ship was in danger of sinking. The privateers decided to return to England, taking White with them. White was **devastated**. He spent the rest of his life trying to return to North America, but he never made it back.

What had happened to the colonists? **Historians** still don't know. However, they have **theories**. Some historians think the Roanoacs may have killed the colonists. Others think the colonists tried to sail to Croatoan Island—or even back home to England. Their ship may have sunk, and all the colonists drowned.

According to another theory, a Spanish ship sailing by the coast of North America could have spotted the English colony. Since England and Spain were at war, the Spanish sailors may have killed the settlers.

Trying to Survive

Some historians have another theory—that the colonists split up and left Roanoke Island in several groups. The colonists were probably weak from lack of food. They were also afraid of being attacked by the Roanoacs. They needed help. Some may have gone south to live with the Croatoans. Others may have gone west or north to find another group of friendly Native Americans to live with.

There is a **legend** that John White's granddaughter, Virginia Dare, lived with the Croatoans and grew up to be a beautiful woman. When she refused to marry a Croatoan with magical powers, he turned her into a white deer.

In 1607, another group of English settlers made its way across the Atlantic Ocean. This group formed a colony called Jamestown, in the present-day state of Virginia. The Jamestown settlers heard stories from Native Americans that the Roanoke colonists had survived. Years later, colonists also heard reports of Native Americans with light gray eyes and blond hair—just like some of the Roanoke colonists had. These could have been children the lost colonists had with Native Americans!

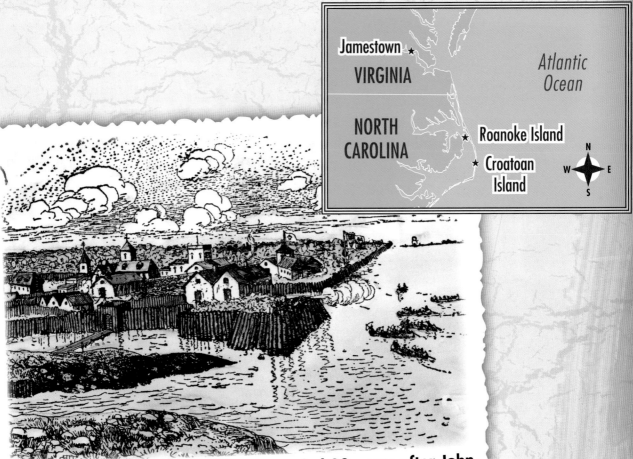

The Jamestown colony (above) was settled 20 years after John White left Roanoke Island to get more supplies. Jamestown became the first successful English colony in North America.

Still Looking for Clues

Unfortunately, no one knows for sure what happened to the lost colonists. None of the theories have been proven true. Yet the search continues. Today, **archaeologists** dig on Roanoke Island and other sites to look for items left behind by the settlers. The things that the archaeologists find may help them learn more about what became of the colonists.

Over hundreds of years, some areas of Roanoke Island have been washed away by storms and ocean waves. Because of this **erosion**, a small part of the colony's original site may be under the water. However, archaeologists have been able to find some objects buried in the sand in the ocean.

Archaeologists digging on Roanoke Island have found items from the 1500s, including pottery, glass, bricks, and beads.

Today, people can visit Roanoke to learn about the abandoned colony. A museum on the island shows how English colonists and Native Americans lived long ago. Visitors can also watch a play called *The Lost Colony*. In it, actors tell the story of the journey John White and the other settlers made to North America. More than 400 years after the disappearance of the colonists, people are still fascinated by the mystery of what happened on Roanoke Island.

The play *The Lost Colony* is put on at this outdoor theater at Fort Raleigh National Historic Site, on Roanoke Island.

Roanoke Colony: Then and Now

THEN: A few hundred English colonists and Native Americans lived on Roanoke Island.

NOW: About 7,000 people live on Roanoke Island.

THEN: Roanoke was the first English colony in North America.

NOW: The colony of Roanoke no longer exists. Roanoke Island is part of North Carolina, in the United States of America.

NORTH CAROLINA

★ Roanoke Island

NOW: It takes about eight hours to fly from England to North Carolina by airplane.

THEN: It could take three months to sail from England to North America.

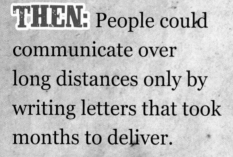

THEN: People could communicate over long distances only by writing letters that took months to deliver.

NOW: People can communicate instantly with phones and computers.

THEN: No one knew what happened to the lost colonists of Roanoke.

NOW: Experts still aren't sure what happened to the lost colonists.

GLOSSARY

abandoned (uh-BAN-duhnd) empty, no longer used

ambush (AM-bush) a surprise attack

archaeologists (ar-kee-OL-uh-jists) scientists who learn about ancient times by studying things they dig up, such as old buildings, tools, and pottery

colony (KOL-uh-nee) an area that has been settled by people from another country and is ruled by that country

desperate (DESS-pur-it) feeling hopeless; willing to do anything to fix an urgent situation

devastated (DEV-uh-*stay*-tid) overwhelmed by a strong negative emotion

erosion (i-ROH-zhuhn) the slow wearing away of land by wind, water, or other natural processes

fort (FORT) a strong building from which people can defend an area from attacks

frantic (FRAN-tik) extremely fearful and worried

governor (GUV-ur-nur) the leader of a group living in an area such as a state or colony

historians (his-TOR-ee-uhnz) people who study past events

legend (LEJ-uhnd) a story from the past that may not be entirely true

Native American (NAY-tiv uh-MER-uh-kin) a member of the first group of people to live in America

natural resources (NACH-ur-uhl REE-*sorss*-iz) materials found in nature that are useful to people

New World (NOO WURLD) the Western Hemisphere, including North America and South America

permanent (PERM-uh-nuhnt) lasting or intending to last for a very long time; not temporary or changing

privateers (prye-vuh-TEERZ) sailors with armed ships who are allowed by their government to attack ships of an enemy country

rivals (RYE-vuhlz) people who compete against each other

settlers (SET-luhrz) people who go to live and make their homes in a new place

shore (SHOR) the land along the edge of a lake, river, or ocean

stranded (STRAND-id) left in a dangerous or unfamiliar place

tension (TEN-shuhn) a state of unfriendliness between people

theories (THIHR-eez) ideas that explain certain facts or events

warriors (WOR-ee-urz) fighters

BIBLIOGRAPHY

Basu, Tanya. "Have We Found the Lost Colony of Roanoke Island?" *National Geographic* (December 6, 2013).

Horn, James. *A Kingdom Strange: The Brief and Tragic History of the Lost Colony of Roanoke*. New York: Basic Books (2010).

Kupperman, Karen Ordahl. *Roanoke: The Abandoned Colony*. New York: Rowman & Littlefield (2007).

READ MORE

Fritz, Jean. *The Lost Colony of Roanoke*. New York: Penguin Books (2004).

Niz, Xavier. *The Mystery of the Roanoke Colony (Graphic Library)*. Mankato, MN: Capstone (2007).

Yolen, Jane, and Heidi E. Y. Stemple. *Roanoke: The Lost Colony—An Unsolved Mystery from History*. New York: Simon & Schuster (2003).

LEARN MORE ONLINE

To learn more about Roanoke, visit
www.bearportpublishing.com/Abandoned

INDEX

ABOUT THE AUTHOR

Kevin Blake has written several books for children.
He lives in Portland, Oregon, with his wife, Melissa, and son, Sam.